✯ How
3+3 Stars for Me!

<u>KIDS</u>: ANSWER THE 3 QUESTIONS EACH DAY. COLOR IN YOUR STARS WHEN YOU ARE DONE.

THEN, FIND SOMEONE TO BE YOUR FAN FOR THE DAY. IT CAN BE A PARENT, SIBLING, COACH, TEACHER, BABYSITTER, GRANDPARENT, NEIGHBOR, OR ANYONE!

<u>FANS</u>: WITHOUT PEEKING AT THE CHILD'S RESPONSES, ANSWER THE 3 QUESTIONS EACH DAY. KIDS GET TO COLOR IN THEIR STARS AS THEY READ YOUR KIND WORDS.

A Note to Adults From the Author

SET UP A REGULAR TIME FOR COMPLETING THIS JOURNAL EACH DAY TO MAKE IT A HABIT.

TRY TO WRITE A <u>DIFFERENT</u> RESPONSE EACH DAY. AVOID REPEATING YOUR ANSWERS.

EVEN THE LITTLEST MOMENTS COUNT! IF YOU ARE FEELING STUCK, SEE THE NEXT PAGE FOR SOME EXAMPLES.

PERHAPS IT WAS A HARD DAY, OR MAYBE THINGS DIDN'T GO SO WELL. YOU SHOULD STILL FILL OUT THIS JOURNAL DAILY. IT IS IMPORTANT TO FIND THE BRIGHT SPOTS, EVEN WHEN IT SEEMS IMPOSSIBLE.

Dr. Lori Fishman

EXAMPLES BY OTHER KIDS

SOMETHING I DID WELL TODAY WAS:

I asked a new kid at school to play with me at recess.

I WAS PROUD OF MYSELF WHEN:

I picked up litter from the playground even though it was kind of gross!

SOMETHING FUN THAT HAPPENED TODAY WAS:

I made up a dance routine and put on a show for my parents.

EXAMPLES BY OTHER FANS

SOMETHING THAT I SAW YOU DO WELL TODAY :

You were very helpful when you put your dish in the sink the first time I asked.

I WAS PROUD OF YOU WHEN:

You showed me the awesome drawing you did in your sketch book today.

ONE THING THAT MAKES YOU SHINE IS:

When you tell funny jokes and they make me laugh.

DATE: _____ TIME: _____

MY 3 STARS TODAY

SOMETHING THAT I DID WELL TODAY WAS:

☆ _____
_____
_____

I WAS PROUD OF MYSELF WHEN:

☆ _____
_____
_____

SOMETHING FUN THAT HAPPENED TODAY WAS:

☆ _____
_____
_____

NOW TURN THE PAGE AND HAND THIS TO YOUR FAN!

MY 3 STARS <u>FOR YOU</u> TODAY

SOMETHING I SAW YOU DO WELL TODAY WAS:

☆ _____
_____
_____

I WAS PROUD OF YOU WHEN:

☆ _____
_____
_____

ONE THING THAT MAKES YOU SHINE IS:

☆ _____
_____
_____

DATE: _____ TIME: _____

MY 3 STARS TODAY

ONE GREAT THING ABOUT ME IS:

_____
_____
_____

I HELPED SOMEONE TODAY BY:

_____
_____
_____

SOMETHING SILLY THAT HAPPENED TODAY WAS:

_____
_____
_____

NOW TURN THE PAGE AND HAND THIS TO YOUR FAN!

FAN'S NAME: _____

MY 3 STARS <u>FOR YOU</u> TODAY

I SAW YOU MAKE THIS GREAT CHOICE TODAY:

_____
_____
_____

IT MADE ME SMILE WHEN YOU:

_____
_____
_____

SOMETHING THAT I ENJOYED DOING WITH YOU:

_____
_____
_____

DATE: _____   TIME: _____

MY 3 STARS TODAY

I TRIED MY BEST TODAY WHEN:

_____
_____
_____

SOMETHING I'M EXCITED ABOUT IS:

_____
_____
_____

A GOOD THING THAT HAPPENED TODAY WAS:

_____
_____
_____

NOW TURN THE PAGE AND HAND THIS TO YOUR FAN!

FAN'S NAME: _____

MY 3 STARS <u>FOR YOU</u> TODAY

I NOTICED YOU TRIED REALLY HARD WHEN:

_____
_____
_____

I WAS IMPRESSED TODAY WHEN YOU:

_____
_____
_____

SOMETHING AWESOME ABOUT YOU IS:

_____
_____
_____

DATE: _____ TIME: _____

MY 3 STARS TODAY

ONE THING PEOPLE LIKE ABOUT ME IS:

_____
_____
_____

I FELT GOOD ABOUT MYSELF TODAY WHEN:

_____
_____
_____

A GOOD THING THAT HAPPENED TODAY WAS:

_____
_____
_____

NOW TURN THE PAGE AND HAND THIS TO YOUR FAN!

FAN'S NAME: _____

MY 3 STARS <u>FOR YOU</u> TODAY

I SAW YOU OVERCOME THIS CHALLENGE:

☆ _____
_____
_____

SOMETHING KIND THAT YOU DID TODAY:

☆ _____
_____
_____

I REALLY ENJOY THE WAY YOU:

☆ _____
_____
_____

DATE: _____   TIME: _____

MY 3 STARS TODAY

SOMETHING THAT I DID WELL TODAY WAS:

_____
_____
_____

I WAS PROUD OF MYSELF WHEN:

_____
_____
_____

SOMETHING FUN THAT HAPPENED TODAY WAS:

_____
_____
_____

NOW TURN THE PAGE AND HAND THIS TO YOUR FAN!

FAN'S NAME _____

MY 3 STARS <u>FOR YOU</u> TODAY

SOMETHING I SAW YOU DO WELL TODAY WAS:

_____
_____
_____

I WAS PROUD OF YOU WHEN:

_____
_____
_____

ONE THING THAT MAKES YOU SHINE IS:

_____
_____
_____

DATE: _____   TIME: _____

MY 3 STARS TODAY

ONE GREAT THING ABOUT ME IS:

_____
_____
_____

I HELPED SOMEONE TODAY BY:

_____
_____
_____

SOMETHING SILLY THAT HAPPENED TODAY WAS:

_____
_____
_____

NOW TURN THE PAGE AND HAND THIS TO YOUR FAN!

FAN'S NAME: _____

MY 3 STARS <u>FOR YOU</u> TODAY

I SAW YOU MAKE THIS GREAT CHOICE TODAY:

☆ _____
_____
_____

IT MADE ME SMILE WHEN YOU:

☆ _____
_____
_____

SOMETHING THAT I ENJOYED DOING WITH YOU:

☆ _____
_____
_____

DATE: _____ TIME: _____

MY 3 STARS TODAY

I TRIED MY BEST TODAY WHEN:

_____
_____
_____

SOMETHING I'M EXCITED ABOUT IS:

_____
_____
_____

A GOOD THING THAT HAPPENED TODAY WAS:

_____
_____
_____

NOW TURN THE PAGE AND HAND THIS TO YOUR FAN!

FAN'S NAME: _____

MY 3 STARS <u>FOR YOU</u> TODAY

I NOTICED YOU TRIED REALLY HARD WHEN:

_____
_____
_____

I WAS IMPRESSED TODAY WHEN YOU:

_____
_____
_____

SOMETHING AWESOME ABOUT YOU IS:

_____
_____
_____

DATE: _____ TIME: _____

MY 3 STARS TODAY

ONE THING PEOPLE LIKE ABOUT ME IS:

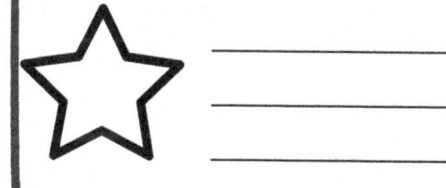
_____
_____
_____

I FELT GOOD ABOUT MYSELF TODAY WHEN:

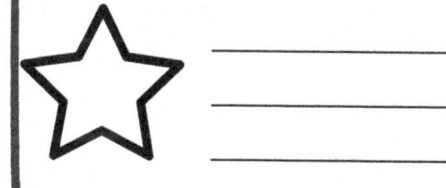
_____
_____
_____

A GOOD THING THAT HAPPENED TODAY WAS:

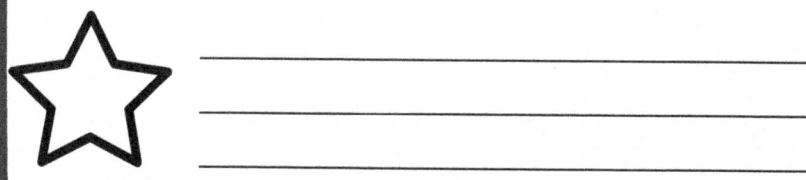
_____
_____
_____

NOW TURN THE PAGE AND HAND THIS TO YOUR FAN!

MY 3 STARS <u>FOR YOU</u> TODAY

I SAW YOU OVERCOME THIS CHALLENGE:

_____
_____
_____

SOMETHING KIND THAT YOU DID TODAY:

_____
_____
_____

I REALLY ENJOY THE WAY YOU:

_____
_____
_____

DATE: _____ TIME: _____

MY 3 STARS TODAY

SOMETHING THAT I DID WELL TODAY WAS:

_____
_____
_____

I WAS PROUD OF MYSELF WHEN:

_____
_____
_____

SOMETHING FUN THAT HAPPENED TODAY WAS:

_____
_____
_____

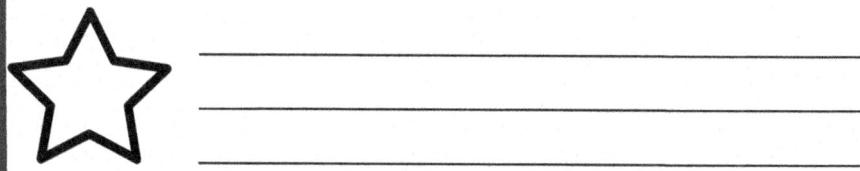

NOW TURN THE PAGE AND HAND THIS TO YOUR FAN!

FAN'S NAME _____

MY 3 STARS <u>FOR YOU</u> TODAY

SOMETHING I SAW YOU DO WELL TODAY WAS:

☆ _____
_____
_____

I WAS PROUD OF YOU WHEN:

☆ _____
_____
_____

ONE THING THAT MAKES YOU SHINE IS:

☆ _____
_____
_____

DATE: _____ TIME: _____

MY 3 STARS TODAY

ONE GREAT THING ABOUT ME IS:

_____
_____
_____

I HELPED SOMEONE TODAY BY:

_____
_____
_____

SOMETHING SILLY THAT HAPPENED TODAY WAS:

_____
_____
_____

NOW TURN THE PAGE AND HAND THIS TO YOUR FAN!

FAN'S NAME: _____

MY 3 STARS <u>FOR YOU</u> TODAY

I SAW YOU MAKE THIS GREAT CHOICE TODAY:

☆ _____
_____
_____

IT MADE ME SMILE WHEN YOU:

☆ _____
_____
_____

SOMETHING THAT I ENJOYED DOING WITH YOU:

☆ _____
_____
_____

DATE: _____   TIME: _____

MY 3 STARS TODAY

I TRIED MY BEST TODAY WHEN:

_____
_____
_____

SOMETHING I'M EXCITED ABOUT IS:

_____
_____
_____

A GOOD THING THAT HAPPENED TODAY WAS:

_____
_____
_____

NOW TURN THE PAGE AND HAND THIS TO YOUR FAN!

FAN'S NAME: _____

MY 3 STARS <u>FOR YOU</u> TODAY

I NOTICED YOU TRIED REALLY HARD WHEN:

_____
_____
_____

I WAS IMPRESSED TODAY WHEN YOU:

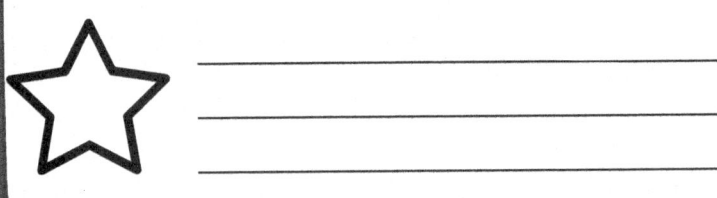

_____
_____
_____

SOMETHING AWESOME ABOUT YOU IS:

_____
_____
_____

DATE: _____ TIME: _____

MY 3 STARS TODAY

ONE THING PEOPLE LIKE ABOUT ME IS:

_____
_____
_____

I FELT GOOD ABOUT MYSELF TODAY WHEN:

_____
_____
_____

A GOOD THING THAT HAPPENED TODAY WAS:

_____
_____
_____

NOW TURN THE PAGE AND HAND THIS TO YOUR FAN!

FAN'S NAME: _____

MY 3 STARS <u>FOR YOU</u> TODAY

I SAW YOU OVERCOME THIS CHALLENGE:

_____
_____
_____

SOMETHING KIND THAT YOU DID TODAY:

_____
_____
_____

I REALLY ENJOY THE WAY YOU:

_____
_____
_____

DATE: _____   TIME: _____

MY 3 STARS TODAY

SOMETHING THAT I DID WELL TODAY WAS:

_____
_____
_____

I WAS PROUD OF MYSELF WHEN:

_____
_____
_____

SOMETHING FUN THAT HAPPENED TODAY WAS:

_____
_____
_____

NOW TURN THE PAGE AND HAND THIS TO YOUR FAN!

FAN'S NAME _____

MY 3 STARS <u>FOR YOU</u> TODAY

SOMETHING I SAW YOU DO WELL TODAY WAS:

☆ _____
_____
_____

I WAS PROUD OF YOU WHEN:

☆ _____
_____
_____

ONE THING THAT MAKES YOU SHINE IS:

☆ _____
_____
_____

DATE: _____   TIME: _____

MY 3 STARS TODAY

ONE GREAT THING ABOUT ME IS:

_____
_____
_____

I HELPED SOMEONE TODAY BY:

_____
_____
_____

SOMETHING SILLY THAT HAPPENED TODAY WAS:

_____
_____
_____

NOW TURN THE PAGE AND HAND THIS TO YOUR FAN!

FAN'S NAME: _____

MY 3 STARS <u>FOR YOU</u> TODAY

I SAW YOU MAKE THIS GREAT CHOICE TODAY:

☆ _____
_____
_____

IT MADE ME SMILE WHEN YOU:

☆ _____
_____
_____

SOMETHING THAT I ENJOYED DOING WITH YOU:

☆ _____
_____
_____

DATE: _____   TIME: _____

MY 3 STARS TODAY

I TRIED MY BEST TODAY WHEN:

_____
_____
_____

SOMETHING I'M EXCITED ABOUT IS:

_____
_____
_____

A GOOD THING THAT HAPPENED TODAY WAS:

_____
_____
_____

NOW TURN THE PAGE AND HAND THIS TO YOUR FAN!

FAN'S NAME: _____

MY 3 STARS <u>FOR YOU</u> TODAY

I NOTICED YOU TRIED REALLY HARD WHEN:

☆ _____
_____
_____

I WAS IMPRESSED TODAY WHEN YOU:

☆ _____
_____
_____

SOMETHING AWESOME ABOUT YOU IS:

☆ _____
_____
_____

DATE: _____ TIME: _____

MY 3 STARS TODAY

ONE THING PEOPLE LIKE ABOUT ME IS:

_____
_____
_____

I FELT GOOD ABOUT MYSELF TODAY WHEN:

_____
_____
_____

A GOOD THING THAT HAPPENED TODAY WAS:

_____
_____
_____

NOW TURN THE PAGE AND HAND THIS TO YOUR FAN!

MY 3 STARS <u>FOR YOU</u> TODAY

I SAW YOU OVERCOME THIS CHALLENGE:

☆ _____
_____
_____

SOMETHING KIND THAT YOU DID TODAY:

☆ _____
_____
_____

I REALLY ENJOY THE WAY YOU:

☆ _____
_____
_____

DATE: _____ TIME: _____

MY 3 STARS TODAY

SOMETHING THAT I DID WELL TODAY WAS:

_____
_____
_____

I WAS PROUD OF MYSELF WHEN:

_____
_____
_____

SOMETHING FUN THAT HAPPENED TODAY WAS:

_____
_____
_____

NOW TURN THE PAGE AND HAND THIS TO YOUR FAN!

MY 3 STARS <u>FOR YOU</u> TODAY

SOMETHING I SAW YOU DO WELL TODAY WAS:

_____

_____

_____

I WAS PROUD OF YOU WHEN:

_____

_____

_____

ONE THING THAT MAKES YOU SHINE IS:

_____

_____

_____

DATE: _____ TIME: _____

MY 3 STARS TODAY

ONE GREAT THING ABOUT ME IS:

_____
_____
_____

I HELPED SOMEONE TODAY BY:

_____
_____
_____

SOMETHING SILLY THAT HAPPENED TODAY WAS:

_____
_____
_____

NOW TURN THE PAGE AND HAND THIS TO YOUR FAN!

FAN'S NAME: _____

MY 3 STARS <u>FOR YOU</u> TODAY

I SAW YOU MAKE THIS GREAT CHOICE TODAY:

_____
_____
_____

IT MADE ME SMILE WHEN YOU:

_____
_____
_____

SOMETHING THAT I ENJOYED DOING WITH YOU:

_____
_____
_____

DATE: _____ TIME: _____

MY 3 STARS TODAY

I TRIED MY BEST TODAY WHEN:

_____
_____
_____

SOMETHING I'M EXCITED ABOUT IS:

_____
_____
_____

A GOOD THING THAT HAPPENED TODAY WAS:

_____
_____
_____

NOW TURN THE PAGE AND HAND THIS TO YOUR FAN!

FAN'S NAME: _____

MY 3 STARS <u>FOR YOU</u> TODAY

I NOTICED YOU TRIED REALLY HARD WHEN:

_____
_____
_____

I WAS IMPRESSED TODAY WHEN YOU:

_____
_____
_____

SOMETHING AWESOME ABOUT YOU IS:

_____
_____
_____

DATE: _____ TIME: _____

MY 3 STARS TODAY

ONE THING PEOPLE LIKE ABOUT ME IS:

_____
_____
_____

I FELT GOOD ABOUT MYSELF TODAY WHEN:

_____
_____
_____

A GOOD THING THAT HAPPENED TODAY WAS:

_____
_____
_____

NOW TURN THE PAGE AND HAND THIS TO YOUR FAN!

FAN'S NAME: _____

MY 3 STARS <u>FOR YOU</u> TODAY

I SAW YOU OVERCOME THIS CHALLENGE:

☆ _____
_____
_____

SOMETHING KIND THAT YOU DID TODAY:

☆ _____
_____
_____

I REALLY ENJOY THE WAY YOU:

☆ _____
_____
_____

DATE: _____ TIME: _____

MY 3 STARS TODAY

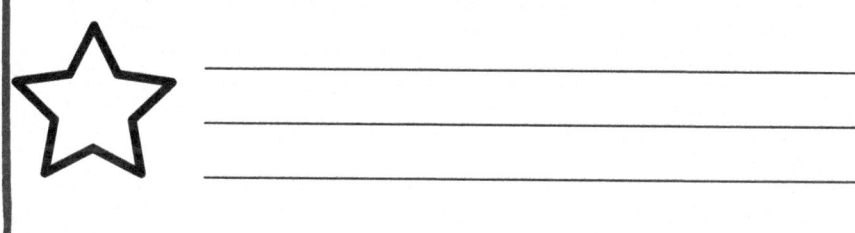

SOMETHING THAT I DID WELL TODAY WAS:

_____
_____
_____

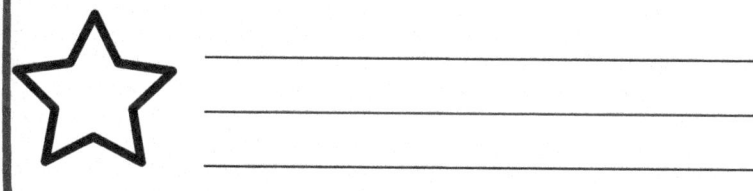

I WAS PROUD OF MYSELF WHEN:

_____
_____
_____

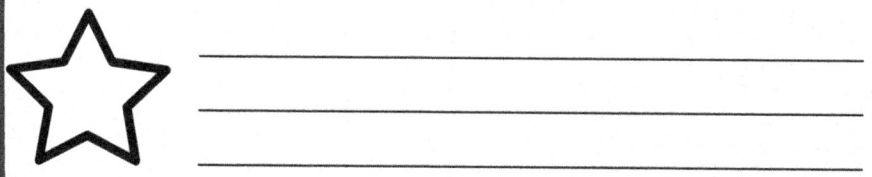

SOMETHING FUN THAT HAPPENED TODAY WAS:

_____
_____
_____

NOW TURN THE PAGE AND HAND THIS TO YOUR FAN!

FAN'S NAME _____

MY 3 STARS <u>FOR YOU</u> TODAY

SOMETHING I SAW YOU DO WELL TODAY WAS:

☆ _____
_____
_____

I WAS PROUD OF YOU WHEN:

☆ _____
_____
_____

ONE THING THAT MAKES YOU SHINE IS:

☆ _____
_____
_____

DATE: _____   TIME: _____

MY 3 STARS TODAY

ONE GREAT THING ABOUT ME IS:

_____
_____
_____

I HELPED SOMEONE TODAY BY:

_____
_____
_____

SOMETHING SILLY THAT HAPPENED TODAY WAS:

_____
_____
_____

NOW TURN THE PAGE AND HAND THIS TO YOUR FAN!

MY 3 STARS <u>FOR YOU</u> TODAY

I SAW YOU MAKE THIS GREAT CHOICE TODAY:

☆ _____
_____
_____

IT MADE ME SMILE WHEN YOU:

☆ _____
_____
_____

SOMETHING THAT I ENJOYED DOING WITH YOU:

☆ _____
_____
_____

DATE: _____ TIME: _____

MY 3 STARS TODAY

I TRIED MY BEST TODAY WHEN:

_____
_____
_____

SOMETHING I'M EXCITED ABOUT IS:

_____
_____
_____

A GOOD THING THAT HAPPENED TODAY WAS:

_____
_____
_____

NOW TURN THE PAGE AND HAND THIS TO YOUR FAN!

FAN'S NAME: _____

MY 3 STARS <u>FOR YOU</u> TODAY

I NOTICED YOU TRIED REALLY HARD WHEN:

_____
_____
_____

I WAS IMPRESSED TODAY WHEN YOU:

_____
_____
_____

SOMETHING AWESOME ABOUT YOU IS:

_____
_____
_____

DATE: _____ TIME: _____

MY 3 STARS TODAY

ONE THING PEOPLE LIKE ABOUT ME IS:

☆ _____
_____
_____

I FELT GOOD ABOUT MYSELF TODAY WHEN:

☆ _____
_____
_____

A GOOD THING THAT HAPPENED TODAY WAS:

☆ _____
_____
_____

NOW TURN THE PAGE AND HAND THIS TO YOUR FAN!

MY 3 STARS <u>FOR YOU</u> TODAY

I SAW YOU OVERCOME THIS CHALLENGE:

_____
_____
_____

SOMETHING KIND THAT YOU DID TODAY:

_____
_____
_____

I REALLY ENJOY THE WAY YOU:

_____
_____
_____

DATE: _____ TIME: _____

MY 3 STARS TODAY

SOMETHING THAT I DID WELL TODAY WAS:

_____
_____
_____

I WAS PROUD OF MYSELF WHEN:

_____
_____
_____

SOMETHING FUN THAT HAPPENED TODAY WAS:

_____
_____
_____

NOW TURN THE PAGE AND HAND THIS TO YOUR FAN!

FAN'S NAME _____

MY 3 STARS <u>FOR YOU</u> TODAY

SOMETHING I SAW YOU DO WELL TODAY WAS:

☆ _____
_____
_____

I WAS PROUD OF YOU WHEN:

☆ _____
_____
_____

ONE THING THAT MAKES YOU SHINE IS:

☆ _____
_____
_____

DATE: _____ TIME: _____

MY 3 STARS TODAY

ONE GREAT THING ABOUT ME IS:

_____
_____
_____

I HELPED SOMEONE TODAY BY:

_____
_____
_____

SOMETHING SILLY THAT HAPPENED TODAY WAS:

_____
_____
_____

NOW TURN THE PAGE AND HAND THIS TO YOUR FAN!

FAN'S NAME: _____

MY 3 STARS <u>FOR YOU</u> TODAY

I SAW YOU MAKE THIS GREAT CHOICE TODAY:

☆ _____
_____
_____

IT MADE ME SMILE WHEN YOU:

☆ _____
_____
_____

SOMETHING THAT I ENJOYED DOING WITH YOU:

☆ _____
_____
_____

DATE: _____ TIME: _____

MY 3 STARS TODAY

I TRIED MY BEST TODAY WHEN:

_____
_____
_____

SOMETHING I'M EXCITED ABOUT IS:

_____
_____
_____

A GOOD THING THAT HAPPENED TODAY WAS:

_____
_____
_____

NOW TURN THE PAGE AND HAND THIS TO YOUR FAN!

FAN'S NAME: _____

MY 3 STARS <u>FOR YOU</u> TODAY

I NOTICED YOU TRIED REALLY HARD WHEN:

_____
_____
_____

I WAS IMPRESSED TODAY WHEN YOU:

_____
_____
_____

SOMETHING AWESOME ABOUT YOU IS:

_____
_____
_____

DATE: _____ TIME: _____

MY 3 STARS TODAY

ONE THING PEOPLE LIKE ABOUT ME IS:

_____
_____
_____

I FELT GOOD ABOUT MYSELF TODAY WHEN:

_____
_____
_____

A GOOD THING THAT HAPPENED TODAY WAS:

_____
_____
_____

NOW TURN THE PAGE AND HAND THIS TO YOUR FAN!

FAN'S NAME: _____

MY 3 STARS <u>FOR YOU</u> TODAY

I SAW YOU OVERCOME THIS CHALLENGE:

☆ _____
_____
_____

SOMETHING KIND THAT YOU DID TODAY:

☆ _____
_____
_____

I REALLY ENJOY THE WAY YOU:

☆ _____
_____
_____

DATE: _____   TIME: _____

MY 3 STARS TODAY

SOMETHING THAT I DID WELL TODAY WAS:

_____
_____
_____

I WAS PROUD OF MYSELF WHEN:

_____
_____
_____

SOMETHING FUN THAT HAPPENED TODAY WAS:

_____
_____
_____

NOW TURN THE PAGE AND HAND THIS TO YOUR FAN!

FAN'S NAME _____

MY 3 STARS <u>FOR YOU</u> TODAY

SOMETHING I SAW YOU DO WELL TODAY WAS:

☆ _____
_____
_____

I WAS PROUD OF YOU WHEN:

☆ _____
_____
_____

ONE THING THAT MAKES YOU SHINE IS:

☆ _____
_____
_____

DATE: _____ TIME: _____

MY 3 STARS TODAY

ONE GREAT THING ABOUT ME IS:

_____
_____
_____

I HELPED SOMEONE TODAY BY:

_____
_____
_____

SOMETHING SILLY THAT HAPPENED TODAY WAS:

_____
_____
_____

NOW TURN THE PAGE AND HAND THIS TO YOUR FAN!

FAN'S NAME: _____

MY 3 STARS <u>FOR YOU</u> TODAY

I SAW YOU MAKE THIS GREAT CHOICE TODAY:

☆ _____
_____
_____

IT MADE ME SMILE WHEN YOU:

☆ _____
_____
_____

SOMETHING THAT I ENJOYED DOING WITH YOU:

☆ _____
_____
_____

You Did It!

NOW GO BACK AND LOOK
AT ALL THOSE STARS
ANY TIME YOU ARE FEELING DOWN.
SEE HOW BRIGHT YOU SHINE!